D0572944

TAKING

RESPONSIBILITY

A Teen's Guide to
Contraception and Pregnancy

The Science of Health:
Youth and Well-Being

Taking Responsibility
A Teen's Guide to Contraception and Pregnancy

Staying Safe
A Teen's Guide to Sexually Transmitted Diseases

What Do I Have to Lose?
A Teen's Guide to Weight Management

Balancing Act
A Teen's Guide to Managing Stress

Surviving the Roller Coaster
A Teen's Guide to Coping with Moods

Clearing the Haze
A Teen's Guide to Smoking-Related Health Issues

Right on Schedule!
A Teen's Guide to Growth and Development

The Best You Can Be
A Teen's Guide to Fitness and Nutrition

The Silent Cry
Teen Suicide and Self-Destructive Behaviors

Breathe Easy!
A Teen's Guide to Allergies and Asthma

Can I Change the Way I Look?
A Teen's Guide to the Health Implications of
Cosmetic Surgery, Makeovers, and Beyond

Taking Care of Your Smile
A Teen's Guide to Dental Care

Dead on Their Feet
Teen Sleep Deprivation and Its Consequences

Dying for Acceptance
A Teen's Guide to Drug- and Alcohol-Related Health Issues

For All to See
A Teen's Guide to Healthy Skin

Taking Responsibility

A Teen's Guide to Contraception and Pregnancy

by Donna Lange

Mason Crest Publishers

Philadelphia

Mason Crest Publishers Inc.
370 Reed Road, Broomall, Pennsylvania 19008
(866) MCP-BOOK (toll free)
www.masoncrest.com

ISBN 1-59084-840-3 (series)

Library of Congress Cataloging-in-Publication Data

Lange, Donna.
  Taking responsibility : a teen's guide to contraception and preg-nancy / by Donna Lange.
     p. cm. — (The science of health : youth and well being)
  Includes bibliographical references and index.
  ISBN 1-59084-841-1
  1. Sex instruction for teenagers—Juvenile literature. 2. Teenage pregnancy—Juvenile literature. 3. Contraception—Juvenile litera-ture. I. Title. II. Science of health.
  HQ35.L2 2004
  613.9'51—dc22
                         2004008155

First edition, 2005
13 12 11 10 09 08 07 06 05   10 9 8 7 6 5 4 3

Designed and produced by Harding House Publishing Service, Vestal, NY 13850.
www.hardinghousepages.com
Cover design by Benjamin Stewart.
Printed and bound in Malaysia

This book is meant to educate and should not be used as an alterna-tive to appropriate medical care. Its creators have made every effort to ensure that the information presented is accurate and up to date—but this book is not intended to substitute for the help and services of trained medical professionals.

CONTENTS

Introduction 7

1. Male and Female Reproductive Systems 11

2. Abstinence 23

3. Contraception (Birth Control) 33

4. Pregnancy Choices 49

5. First Trimester 63

6. Second and Third Trimesters 75

7. Labor and Delivery 91

8. Parenting or Adoption 105

Further Reading 120

For More Information 122

Glossary 124

Index 126

Picture Credits 127

Biographies 128

INTRODUCTION
by Dr. Sara Forman

You're not a little kid anymore. When you look in the mirror, you probably see a new person, someone who's taller, bigger, with a face that's starting to look more like an adult's than a child's. And the changes you're experiencing on the inside may be even more intense than the ones you see in the mirror. Your emotions are changing, your attitudes are changing, and even the way you think is changing. Your friends are probably more important to you than they used to be, and you no longer expect your parents to make all your decisions for you. You may be asking more questions and posing more challenges to the adults in your life. You might experiment with new identities—new ways of dressing, hairstyles, ways of talking—as you try to determine just who you really are. Your body is maturing sexually, giving you a whole new set of confusing and exciting feelings. Sorting out what is right and wrong for you may seem overwhelming.

Growth and development during adolescence is a multifaceted process involving every aspect of your being. It all happens so fast that it can be confusing and distressing. But this stage of your life is entirely normal. Every adult in your life made it through adolescence—and you will too.

7

Taking Responsibility

But what exactly is adolescence? According to the American Heritage Dictionary, adolescence is "the period of physical and psychological development from the onset of puberty to maturity." What does this really mean?

In essence, adolescence is the time in our lives when the needs of childhood give way to the responsibilities of adulthood. According to psychologist Erik Erikson, these years are a time of separation and individuation. In other words, you are separating from your parents, becoming an individual in your own right. These are the years when you begin to make decisions on your own. You are becoming more self-reliant and less dependent on family members.

When medical professionals look at what's happening physically—what they refer to as the biological model—they define the teen years as a period of hormonal transformation toward sexual maturity, as well as a time of peak growth, second only to the growth during the months of infancy. This physical transformation from childhood to adulthood takes place under the influence of society's norms and social pressures; at the same time your body is changing, the people around you are expecting new things from you. This is what makes adolescence such a unique and challenging time.

Being a teenager in North America today is exciting yet stressful. For those who work with teens, whether by parenting them, educating them, or providing services to them, adolescence can be challenging as well. Youth are struggling with many messages from society and the media about how they should behave and who they should be. "Am I normal?" and "How do I fit in?" are often questions with which teens wrestle. They are facing decisions about their health such as how to take care of their bodies, whether to use drugs and alcohol, or whether to have sex.

This series of books on adolescents' health issues provides teens, their parents, their teachers, and all those who work with them accurate information and the tools to keep them safe and healthy. The topics include information about:

- normal growth
- social pressures
- emotional issues
- specific diseases to which adolescents are prone
- stressors facing youth today
- sexuality

The series is a dynamic set of books, which can be shared by youth and the adults who care for them. By providing this information to educate in these areas, these books will help build a foundation for readers so they can begin to work on improving the health and well-being of youth today.

1

Male and Female Reproductive Systems

"Good morning, ladies and gentlemen. Today's lesson is the human reproductive system," Mr. Mitchell said. "Let's name the reproductive organs."

"I bet I know some you've never heard," Dominic said. A few guys snickered.

"Sir, I remind you that in this class we respect each other," Mr. Mitchell said. "Who knows the correct medical term for a male reproductive organ?"

"The penis. That's spelled P-E-N-I-S," Dominic said.

"Thank you." After Mr. Mitchell listed all the male and female reproductive organs on the blackboard, he passed out worksheets with diagrams. "You can work together or by yourself. Label each organ—using the correct medical term. Then we'll discuss how the female and male reproductive systems work separately and together."

The students worked in small groups. Shawna ignored the guys who bragged they knew all the answers—even about ovulation and menstruation. When class was dismissed, she and Tori walked to their lockers.

"Shawna, hurry up!" Tori tugged at her best friend's arm.

"Sorry."

"Are you still thinking about those reproductive organs?"

"No. It's not like I don't know about sex."

"You don't think Mr. Mitchell would ever ask us about our private lives, do you?"

"I don't know. I don't care if people know about Logan and me." Shawna opened her locker and took out a notebook. "I wish the day wasn't over. I hate going home before Mom gets there. Bill gets on my nerves. When he moved in with us, I thought we would be a real family."

"Blended families need time to adjust," Tori said.

"We aren't blending. As hard as life was with just one parent, that was better than having Bill around."

Tori shrugged. "I'll call you when I get home from work."

"You can tell me all about Carlos. By the way, do you want me to get you something for Friday night? You know, sometimes guys conveniently forget." Shawna rolled her eyes.

"No, I'm okay." Tori waved good-bye.

Having sex is a life-changing experience. Some teenagers choose to have sex, while others wait. Some teenagers don't use contraception and get pregnant, and others get pregnant even using contraception. Pregnant teenagers have difficult decisions to make. Some teenagers choose to give up their babies for adoption, and some teenagers choose to become parents. Before having sex, a person should understand the risks and consequences of these life-changing decisions. This understanding begins with knowledge of how the reproductive system works.

The Male Body

The reproduction system is a set of organs that make it possible for a couple to reproduce. The sex organs of a male are different than a female's, and each organ has a different function. A male's reproductive organs are located both outside and inside his body. The ***genitals*** are the penis and the scrotum. The penis is made of spongy tissue and blood vessels. It is shaped like a tube and consists of two parts: the shaft, which becomes hard during erections; and the rounded tip, called the glans (sometimes called the tip or the head). The penis contains the urethra, the channel that carries urine out of the body. In

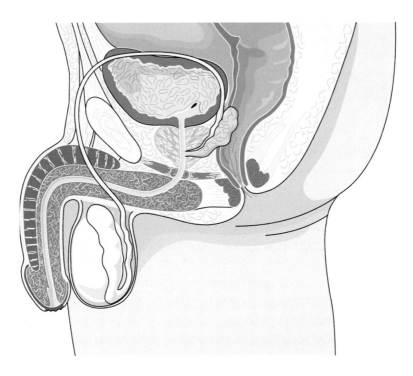

The male reproductive system.

the process called ejaculation, semen is released through the urethra. Also, the penis is a source of sexual pleasure.

Did you know?

- Once a sperm enters an egg, that egg is sealed off from further contact and no other sperm can unite with it.
- Sperm cells are solids that swim in semen.
- Sperm cells are so small that several million could fit on the head of a pin. They can only be seen with a microscope.
- It takes only one sperm to fertilize an egg.

The scrotum is the flexible bag of wrinkly skin that covers and protects the two testicles or testes. In order to produce sperm, the testicles must be kept at a temperature a little lower than body temperature, so the testicles normally hang away from the body. During **puberty**, males start making sex cells. The hormone testosterone is released and causes sperm cells to mature inside the testicles.

Each testicle is connected to a small tube-like structure called the epididymis. Sperm cells travel from each testicle, through the epididymis to the vas deferens. The two vas deferens, sometimes called sperm ducts, are narrow tubes that deliver sperm from the testicles to the seminal vesicles for storage until ejaculation. Each tube starts at the epididymis and winds all the way to the urethra. The two seminal vesicles and the prostate gland produce fluids that combine with the sperm to create a mixture called semen. The urethra is part of the urinary

Sperm swimming toward an egg.

system. This tube carries urine from the bladder, to the penis, and out through the opening of the penis. The urethra is also the passageway for semen. As sperm travel, they mature to be able to fertilize a female's egg. The sperm travel along in the fluids to and through the urethra. Semen also leaves the body via the urethra.

Once a male's body begins to produce sperm, he will usually continue to produce sperm for the rest of his life. Millions of sperm are produced each day. If not ejaculated, the body absorbs the sperm.

The Female Body

Like the male reproductive system, some of the female's sex organs are on the outside of the body, while others are located inside the body. The breasts are located on the upper part of the body. These organs provide nourishment for babies. They contain the mammary glands, which produce breast milk during and after pregnancy.

The whole area of soft skin between a female's legs is called the vulva. The vulva covers the entire genital area of the labia, the clitoris, the opening to the urethra, and the opening to the vagina. The labia are two sets of soft folds of skin inside the vulva. The clitoris is a small mound of skin about the size of a pea, and its purpose is sexual pleasure. The urethra is not one of the female's sex organs. It is a tube with a small opening through which urine leaves the body. The vagina is between the uterus and the outside of the female body. Also, the vagina is the passageway for menstrual flow and the opening for sexual intercourse. The opening to the vagina is bigger than the opening to the urethra.

Inside the female abdomen are two ovaries, two fallopian tubes, the uterus, and the vagina. One ovary is on

Q: Do urine and menstrual fluid leave a woman's body through the same opening?

A: No. During a period, menstrual fluid leaves the body through the vagina. Urine is released through the urethra.

17

> Some females may begin to release eggs even before they start to menstruate. This means that although it is rare, it is possible for a female to become pregnant before she has started to menstruate.

each side of the uterus. The ovaries contain a female's sex cells—also called eggs or ova. A single egg is called an ovum. Females are born with millions of eggs in each ovary, but the eggs do not begin maturing until puberty. The two fallopian tubes are channels that lead from the ovaries to the uterus. One end of each tube almost touches an ovary, while the other end of each tube is connected to the uterus.

The uterus is the place where a developing baby grows for about nine months until it is ready to be born. Sometimes called the womb, the uterus stretches as the fetus grows bigger. The uterus is made of strong muscles and is hollow inside. It is about the size and shape of a small upside-down pear and is connected to both fallopian tubes and the inside end of the vagina.

The vagina leads from the uterus to the outside of the female body. A baby travels through the vagina when it is ready to be born. The vagina is also the passageway through which a small amount of blood, other fluids, and tissue leave the uterus, about once a

LATIN LESSON

Labia is the Latin word for *lips*.
Vulva comes from the Latin word *volva*, which means covering.
Semen is the Latin word for *seed*.

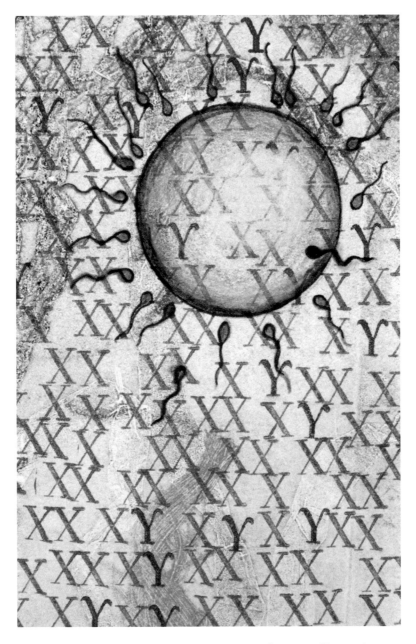

Conception occurs when a sperm penetrates the egg cell's membrane.

month. This small amount of normal bleeding is called menstruation, or "having a period," and begins when a girl reaches puberty. The vagina is also the place where the penis fits during sexual intercourse.

The cervix is a small opening located in the lower part of the uterus. It extends into the top of the vagina. This opening is the entrance to the uterus and fallopian tubes, so sperm travel up through the cervix. The cervix is the exit from the uterus for menstrual flow.

Ovulation

At the start of puberty, the ovaries begin to produce the hormones estrogen and progesterone. About once a month, the ovaries release a single mature egg. In her life, a female will release about four hundred to five hundred eggs. This periodic release of a mature egg from an ovary is called ovulation. At about the same time every month, when an egg is released from one of the ovaries, it is

In males, puberty can begin any time from about age ten to about fifteen. During this time, males begin to produce sex cells and continue making sex cells until old age.

In females, puberty can begin any time from about age nine to about fourteen. During this time, menstruation begins—female eggs begin to mature and be released. After a woman is about fifty, her egg cells are no longer able to produce babies.

swept into one of the fallopian tubes, where it begins to travel to the uterus. If the egg is not fertilized, it is discharged from the body as part of the menstrual flow.

Reproduction

As soon as a female's ovaries have begun to release eggs, she can become pregnant if she has sexual intercourse. Sometimes called mating, sexual intercourse is the sexual joining of two individuals. Sexual intercourse happens when a male's erect penis enters the female's vagina. When the male ejaculates, releasing semen into the female's vagina, millions of sperm travel through the cervix and up a fallopian tube. If an egg is present in the fallopian tube, the egg can become fertilized. Conception is the moment the sperm fertilizes the egg. The fertilized egg then travels through the fallopian tube into the uterus, and attaches itself to the wall of the uterus. The female is pregnant and the united cell can develop into a baby.

2
ABSTINENCE

Mr. Mitchell introduced to his class the abstinence program director from a local women's health clinic and three college students.

"Thanks for inviting us to share our two-day seminar

on abstinence. We are here to encourage you to make wise choices about your sexuality. We are not here to tell you what to do or to put you on a guilt trip. We want you to consider the cost of having sex and then ask yourself if sex is worth that cost," Ms. Thompson said.

Tori started taking notes.

"Sex is a choice. Sex is not forced. If you're in that situation, that was not your fault, and you should talk with someone about that," Ms. Thompson said.

Tori stopped writing and closed her eyes, trying to push out memories.

Ms. Thompson explained abstinence does not mean sex is bad. She said sex is good, and that's why people want to save it, to make sure they can enjoy it later in life.

24

"But why would any normal guy wait?" Dominic asked.

"People wait because of religious reasons, or they want to protect their emotions, or they don't want to get a sexually transmitted disease, or they don't want to become pregnant

> **Think First**
>
> Think with your head before you act with other parts of your body.

or get their girlfriend pregnant," Ms. Thompson said. "Sex before marriage has risks and consequences. Outside of marriage, sex can change your life. Within the right boundaries, sex is good and you want to protect it."

The college volunteers performed a skit about a couple who had been dating for several months. The guy left notes in his girlfriend's locker. He walked her to classes, and they even talked on the phone for hours.

"The best part of the relationship is that we can talk about everything," the girl said to her best friend. But the girl admitted she hadn't shared everything yet. She didn't know how or when to tell her boyfriend she got herpes as a result of a past relationship. When she finally told him, he was hurt she hadn't told him earlier, and he left her because she had herpes. The class agreed the girl should she have told the guy before the relationship got too serious.

It's never an easy time to tell, Tori thought.

The second day's presentation focused on dating and pressures, and the difference between love and infatuation. One particular skit involved two girls and one guy.

"You mean the world to me," the guy said to one girl. "Here's something I've been saving to give to you. I want you to have it." He gave her a ring box with a piece of gum inside the box.

Taking Responsibility

"Thanks." The girl chewed the gum. "It's good."

Then the guy noticed the other girl.

"Would you wait here for me?" he asked.

While the first girl waited, the guy introduced himself to the second girl. He told the second girl she was important to him and he had a gift he had been saving for her. Then he returned to the first girl and asked for his gum. When she handed him the chewed gum, he put it back in the wrapper and inside the box. He thanked her and said good-bye. When he returned to the second girl and offered her the gum, she refused to accept it.

"Sex is like that gum. There are some things that are best when shared with only one person," Ms. Thompson said. "Many teens regret having sex. But changing is never too late. If you have had sex, you can start over—not biologically, but in your heart and mind. Then some day you can say to that special person, 'I made mistakes, but from this point forward I saved myself for you.'"

Purity Ring or Commitment Ring

A purity ring or a commitment ring is a reminder of a person's commitment to abstain from sex until marriage. For those teens who have already had sex, this ring is a symbol of making a commitment to start over; to abstain from sex from this point until marriage. Some teens celebrate this occasion privately, while other teens participate in a public ceremony. Often, parents give a ring to their daughter or son. This gift encourages the teen to keep the promise of abstinence.

Taking Responsibility

Your body belongs to you. Never let yourself be pressured into sharing it with someone if you're not ready for that kind of intimacy.

28

Ms. Thompson continued talking about *secondary virginity*.

"I have a ten-dollar bill. Does anyone want it?"

Several students raised their hands. Ms. Thompson crumpled the ten-dollar bill.

"Do you want it now?" she asked.

"Yes," the students replied.

"Really?" Ms. Thompson dropped the ten-dollar bill onto the floor and stomped on it. "Would you want it now?"

"Of course," one student said.

"Why? It's all dirty and used. It doesn't look brand new."

"But it's still worth ten dollars," the student said.

"That's right. Its value has not changed. You are like that. It doesn't matter how you've been treated in the past or what choices you've made that you may regret. You still have the same value you did before those experiences," Ms. Thompson said.

At the end of class, Ms. Thompson gave the students her business card and asked them to complete an evaluation form. Tori added a comment at the bottom of her form. *Thank you for showing me that no matter what has happened to me in the past, I am still valuable and worthy of respect.*

For some people, babies arrive before marriage and often before love. By making a lifestyle choice of abstinence, a person can grow relationships

> **True or False?**
>
> "Trust me. I won't get you pregnant."
>
> False. Abstinence is the only guaranteed way to make sure a woman will not get pregnant.

29

before making babies. Abstaining from sex means not having sex at all for a period of time. Some people choose to practice abstinence until marriage. The temptation to have sex outside of marriage is powerful, but people have the strength to say no. A person who abstains has inner strength, self-control, and self-respect. Choosing to say no to sex and following through on that decision show maturity.

> If sex is not a part of a couple's relationship, how can they show love to each other?
>
> - learn a sport or hobby together.
> - write a love poem or note.
> - have their picture taken together.
> - compliment each other.

Premature, uncommitted sex has both emotional and psychological consequences. Some consequences are short term, while others are long term and carry into marriage and parenting. Consequences may be serious and hard to imagine, but they happen. Many teens cry the morning after a sexual experience because they are terrified of becoming pregnant. These teens may also regret their decision about having sex. Regret can last a long time. Many people feel guilty about having sex. Guilt is a strong sense of having done something wrong. Sometimes the guilt comes from hurting other people. A teen may feel guilty because he knows his parents would be disappointed. For some people, having sex before marriage goes against their religious beliefs that sex should be saved for marriage.

Both women and men may suffer a loss of dignity and self-worth when they are in a sexual relationship. Some people feel used or betrayed after the breakup of a sexual relationship, and they can experience difficulty in future relationships. They may develop low self-esteem and seek attention through another short-lived sexual relationship. Other people don't want to get hurt again, so they don't trust. Having sex can lead a person to believe that the relationship was serious, because sex can cause an emotional bond. When that bond is broken, betrayal can turn to anger. The more someone thinks the relationship is based on real love, the deeper the pain if the couple breaks up. Sometimes the emotional pain leads to depression and even suicide.

Whether or not to have sexual intercourse is a decision each person has a right to make. Since most teens have not yet met their lifetime partner, it may be wise to wait before having sex. So how does someone abstain from sex? A person needs to make the choice *before* being in a situation that may lead to sex. Healthy people make healthy choices, including choices about one's body and about sex. Respect for life begins with respecting oneself and one's decisions.

3

CONTRACEPTION (BIRTH CONTROL)

"Good afternoon, ladies and gentlemen," Mr. Mitchell said. "Today's topic is contraception or birth control, which means to control birth or stop it from happening. We have learned that abstinence is the only birth control that is

Taking Responsibility

100 percent effective. But if a couple is going to have sexual intercourse, the couple would be wise to use two methods of contraception. If a guy is prepared, and the girl is prepared, then neither has to depend on the other person. Each person assumes responsibility to prevent a pregnancy."

The students discussed various birth control methods available to teens. Students wanted to know what types of questions would be asked if a teen asked for birth control, and would the teen's parent need to know. Mr. Mitchell explained the cost of each method, whether or not it required a prescription, how much planning was required, and the risks and failure rates of each method.

"Now we're going to talk about your mental wellness. It's safe to say most of you have not met your life partner yet, so waiting to have sex is important," Mr. Mitchell said.

Tori forced herself to pay attention instead of reliving memories.

"What is the best gift I can give my children?" Mr. Mitchell asked.

"Money," a student said.

"Health," another student said.

"Love," a third student replied.

"All those are good answers. I think the best gift I can give my children is when I tell them I love their mother," Mr. Mitchell said.

Shawna was straightening a pile of papers when Bill tossed his coat over a chair.

"You must be sucking up for something. Your mother may be blind, but nothing gets by me." Bill grabbed a beer from the refrigerator. "So what do want this time?"

"Nothing from you!"

"Don't take that tone with me!" Bill shouted.

Taking Responsibility

Shawna walked out of the kitchen.

"Don't walk away from me when I'm talking to you," Bill said.

"You aren't my father. You can't tell me what to do." Shawna walked into her bedroom and slammed the door. After a while, Shawna changed her clothes for her date with Logan. Shawna wanted to please him, so she put on his favorite sweater. She looked in the mirror and smiled. *At least there is one man in this world who loves me*, she thought.

Condoms are one kind of over-the-counter contraception. They even come in different colors!

36

> **Did you know?**
>
> • You can get pregnant even if you stand up while having sex?
> • A girl can get pregnant the first time she has intercourse?
> • Jumping up and down or dancing immediately after sex will not keep a woman from becoming pregnant?
> • A woman can still get pregnant if the man doesn't penetrate? Sperm can still reach a vagina if the penis makes close contact.

Teens who choose to engage in sexual relationships should use birth control or contraception. In order for birth control to be effective, a person must learn how to use contraceptives and must use them every time he or she has sexual intercourse. Other than abstinence, no birth control method is guaranteed to work 100 percent of the time. Birth control methods are based on behavior, barrier, or hormones. Several kinds are available today.

Over-the-Counter Contraception

"Over-the-counter contraceptives" can be purchased at drugstores and department stores. Other types of contraceptives require a prescription or must be fitted by a health care provider. Not every kind of contraceptive is right for every person. An individual should first speak with a health care provider, who can assist in deciding which methods are best.

BEHAVIORAL CONTRACEPTION

Some people prefer to use behavioral methods of birth control. Natural family planning method (NFP) is called natural because there is no pill to take and nothing to put on or insert. NFP is also called the rhythm method because sex is planned according to the rhythm of ovulation. With this type of birth control, a couple determines when the woman's ovary has released an egg, and then the couple abstains from having sexual intercourse during that time. Sometimes ovulation is hard to figure out. A woman must record the dates of her menstrual period, her basal body temperature, and changes she observes to her cervical mucus. She records these changes for a few menstrual cycles.

A woman can become pregnant at any time during the month—even during her period. Having sex before or after ovulation only reduces the chances of pregnancy. NFP is relatively inexpensive and has no dangers or side effects, but it requires a great deal of dedication. This method is not recommended for teens.

The withdrawal method is a popular behavioral birth control method. When a couple uses this method, the male withdraws or removes his penis from the woman's vagina just before the man ejaculates. This method is not a good choice. Droplets of semen filled with sperm cells often leak out before ejaculation. A man may fail to remove his penis before he ejaculates. When he is excited, it is difficult for him to stop in the middle of sex and pull out of the vagina. Sometimes ejaculation occurs suddenly, so the man cannot tell when he should pull out. This method does not work very well.

Hormonal Contraception

Some people use hormone-based contraceptives. Birth control pills (commonly called "the pill") contain artificial hormones that keep ovaries from releasing mature eggs, fooling the body into thinking it is pregnant. For a woman to obtain birth control pills, she must have a prescription from a health care provider. In order for this method to work, the woman must remember to follow the directions of taking the pill each day. While on the pill, some women may develop blood clots, which can cause strokes or heart attacks. The pill can also cause temporary high blood pressure. Smoking and using the pill can increase the risk of stroke.

Another type of hormone-based contraception is the patch. This thin plastic patch is placed on the skin of a

"I forgot" is a lame excuse. Teenagers may get pregnant when they forget:

- to use their birth control consistently.
- to use birth control correctly.
- they can still get pregnant if they have sexual intercourse while they are under the influence of alcohol or drugs.

A pregnancy requires two people. A man who shares getting a woman pregnant also shares taking responsibility for the baby.

woman's stomach, buttocks, upper outer arm, or upper torso. The patch releases combined hormones. This method protects against pregnancy for one month. One advantage of the patch is a woman does not have to take a pill every day. However, disadvantages include possible skin reaction at the site of the patch, menstrual cramps, a change in vision for someone who wears contact lenses, and an increased risk of high blood pressure and stroke.

A month's worth of birth control pills.

Norplant and Depo-Provera are hormone-based birth control devices that work like the pill, but on a long-term basis. A health care provider places Norplant in a female's upper arm just under her skin. It is effective for five years. Depo-Provera is nicknamed "the shot" because it is injected by syringe and needle into the buttock or upper arm. An injection lasts three months, at which time a woman must receive another shot or change to a different method. Norplant and Depo-Provera are reversible, and both methods are extremely effective.

BARRIER METHODS

Barrier methods of contraception are used to prevent sperm from entering the vagina. One popular barrier method is the condom. A condom is a soft, thin cover that fits over an erect penis. It is also called a rubber because condoms are usually made out of a rubbery material called latex. Condoms are designed to trap semen, preventing any from entering a woman's vagina and reaching an egg. When a man ejaculates, semen is kept inside the condom, but sometimes semen can leak out. To prevent pregnancy, a condom works better when used with a spermicide.

Condoms are inexpensive and easy to use. They can be purchased in advance by either a woman or man. Condoms are one size. The elastic material stretches to fit any size penis. A man needs to be careful when putting on a

Some of the earliest condoms were made from dried sheep gut. Those are still known as "skins."

condom because if a condom is pulled too tight, it may rip or tear. A man should learn how to use a condom correctly before he uses it during sex. (He can practice by himself.) It is important to put on the condom as soon as the penis is erect because sperm can slip out of the penis before sex. Also, the penis gets soft soon after an orgasm and the condom can slip off, and sperm can spill into the vagina. Each condom should be used only once and then disposed of properly. A condom should not be flushed down a toilet.

Like other forms of birth control, condoms are not 100 percent effective. They sometimes break. Semen can leak out of the condom. An out-of-date condom can deteriorate or even burst. Condoms can be ruined if they are carried around in a pocket or wallet, or left in a car. If an individual has any doubt about the condition of a condom, he should throw it away and use a new one.

The female condom is a soft pouch-like condom with one closed end that the woman inserts into the vagina before sexual intercourse. The open end remains outside the vagina and is entered by the penis. This contraceptive provides a physical barrier between partners during intercourse. Female condoms do not require fitting by a health care professional. A person can purchase a female condom, which is sold with lubricant, wherever condoms for men are sold. Like condoms for

The History of Condoms

The condom was named for its inventor, a Doctor Condom, court physician to Charles II of England in the seventeenth century. The condom became so famous that the doctor changed his name.

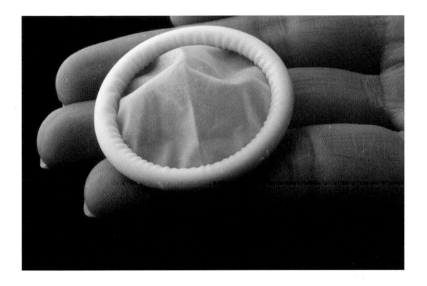

An unused male condom.

men, a female condom should be used only once and then properly discarded.

The diaphragm and the cervical cap are small latex cups that fit inside the vagina and are placed against the cervix before sexual intercourse. The diaphragm covers a woman's cervix, and is kept in place with pelvic structures. It must remain in place for at least six hours after the last act of intercourse. The cervical cap is a small, flexible rubber cap that fits more tightly over the cervix and is used with a spermicide. It is smaller than the diaphragm, and it grips the cervix like a thimble on a finger. The cervical cap is somewhat more difficult than the diaphragm to insert and remove, but it is more convenient. It requires less spermicide or jelly, it can be inserted for a longer amount of time before intercourse, and it can be kept in for up to forty-eight hours.

Taking Responsibility

A woman must visit a health care provider in order to be fitted. She will have to practice inserting either the cervical cap or diaphragm because she cannot see when it is in place. Both the diaphragm and the cervical cap prevent sperm from entering the cervix and traveling to the fallopian tubes. With these types of birth control, a woman needs to use a spermicide, which can be purchased at a drugstore without a prescription. She should add a fresh application of spermicide before each act of sexual intercourse.

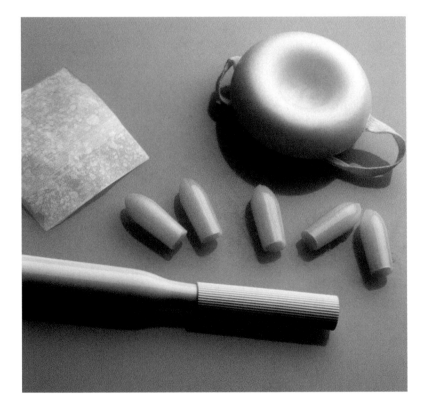

Foams, suppositories, and sponges all use spermicides that help prevent pregancy by blocking or killing the sperm.

44

Is emergency contraception the same as mifepristone? No. Mifepristone is the generic name for RU-486. Mifepristone is not a contraceptive because it is taken after a woman *knows* she is pregnant and with the intention of ending a pregnancy. The so-called "morning-after pill" is sold to women as a form of emergency contraception to prevent pregnancy.

Foams, creams, gels, films, and suppositories are different types of spermicides. They contain an ingredient that blocks or kills sperm on contact. Spermicides are sold without prescription. These types of birth control can be used alone, but they are more effective when used with a barrier method. When they are used alone, they are usually not able to kill, block, or catch every sperm. These types of contraceptives are also inserted into the vagina before sexual intercourse. Spermicide and sponges should be used with a condom or diaphragm. Some spermicides provide protection immediately after insertion, while others require ten to fifteen minutes to melt and spread before intercourse begins. For all spermicides, additional applications are required for each act of intercourse.

An intrauterine device (IUD) is a small object that is placed inside the uterus to prevent an egg from planting itself in the lining of the uterus. The IUD must be inserted and removed by a trained health care professional. It can remain in the uterus for up to ten years. Some health care providers and women believe that the latest IUDs pose risks. Women who have not had children are not ideal candidates for the IUD.

PERMANENT CONTRACEPTION

Permanent contraception is also called sterilization. A vasectomy is permanent contraception for a man. A doctor removes or ties off a small piece of the vas deferens. Then the semen that is ejaculated no longer carries any sperm. Tubal ligation is permanent contraception for a woman. A small piece of each fallopian tube is cut and tied to prevent eggs from meeting sperm and traveling into the uterus. Although these procedures may sometimes be reversed, they should be considered permanent.

EMERGENCY CONTRACEPTION

Postcoital contraception is an emergency method because it must be used promptly *after* unprotected sex. A woman can request emergency contraception when a method of contraception has failed, if she has been raped, or if no method of contraception was used. It is not a substitute for regular contraception, and it is no excuse for taking chances.

The best example of emergency contraception is contraceptive pills, or "morning-after pills." These pills contain hormones that are thought

> When considering using birth control, ask yourself these questions:
>
> - How well does it work?
> - How safe is it to use?
> - How do I need to plan?

46

to prevent fertilization or the planting of a fertilized egg in the lining of the uterus. These pills have risks and significant side effects. Once a woman is pregnant, these pills will not work. This method must take place under the supervision of a health care professional.

An Important Choice

Some individuals believe that using any method of birth control is wrong. Others believe that using a form of natural birth control is okay, but it is wrong to use over-the-counter and prescription birth control methods. No one should wait until he or she is having sex to ask advice about contraception. Both partners are responsible for contraception.

A teen can obtain birth control information from health clinics, family planning clinics, or a school health clinic. If the school doesn't have a clinic, the nurse can refer the student to the proper resource. Also, an individual can find the name of a clinic in the yellow pages of a telephone book. Teens can talk with their parents about birth control and abstinence.

Even when using birth control, having sex can lead to pregnancy. Every time a couple has sexual intercourse it can result in pregnancy—unless the female is already pregnant. The only sure way to avoid pregnancy is abstinence. No matter what anyone says, *sex is never an emergency*.

47

4

PREGNANCY CHOICES

Shawna felt nauseous and exhausted. She forced herself to shower and dress. On the way to school, she nibbled some crackers, hoping that would settle her stomach. After her first class, she went to the school nurse.

Taking Responsibility

"I don't feel well." Shawna sat on a cot.

"What hurts?" the nurse asked. "Do you have a sore throat?"

"My stomach is upset, but I don't vomit."

The nurse took Shawna's temperature and gave her a cold compress for her forehead.

"How long have you been feeling like this?"

"I don't know. At least for a few days. I'm so tired I can hardly stay awake. Is it the flu?"

"Is there any chance you could be pregnant?" the nurse asked.

"I don't think so. Logan hates using condoms, so he convinced me to start taking the pill. I told him I don't always remember, but I take it at least every other day."

"Every other day may not be good enough. Shawna, you should talk with your mother."

"Tell her that I may be pregnant?"

"At least tell her you have not felt well for several days and you should go to the doctor."

"I don't know if I can do that. Her boyfriend will flip."

"How about talking with your father?"

"My father has been gone for years. He sends a check every Christmas. Like that's going to make up for everything."

"If there's a chance you're pregnant, it's important you see a doctor as soon as possible. You may rest here for a while." The nurse pulled the curtain and turned off the light.

Tori and Shawna walked to the women's clinic located across the street from the high school. A receptionist asked Shawna to sign in and wait for a counselor. A few minutes later, a counselor escorted Shawna to a private room. After talking with the counselor, Shawna went to the ladies' room and returned with a sample of urine in a

50

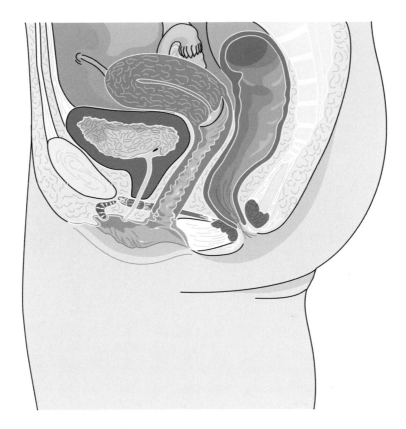

The female reproductive system.

cup. The counselor explained the test, and then Shawna performed the test and waited.

"Shawna, the test is positive." the counselor said.

After talking with the counselor for a while longer, Shawna met Tori in the waiting room. The two friends left the clinic with brochures about unplanned pregnancy, medical services, adoption agencies, and community services.

"How soon do you have to decide?" Tori asked.

51

Taking Responsibility

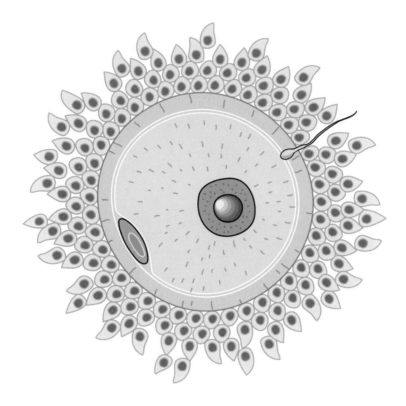

It only takes one sperm cell to start a pregnancy!

"First I have to tell Mom. I don't know how she will react. The counselor said I need a medical exam. I've already made an appointment to see the doctor."

That evening, Shawna waited until Bill left the house.

"Mom, I have something to tell you." Shawna paused. "I'm pregnant."

Her mother didn't cry. She didn't scream. She just sat there. Finally she said, "Shawna, you have three choices. You can have an abortion. You can give up the baby for adoption. You can raise the baby. I'll support whatever decision you make, but I'm not raising your baby. Have you told Logan yet?"

"No. But when I tell him, I'm sure he'll be thrilled because he loves me. We are going to be a real family."

Pregnancy is the period of time before birth during which a fertilized egg plants itself inside the lining of the uterus, grows and eventually develops into a baby.

"My period was always so regular, that if it arrived two hours late, I knew I was pregnant," one mother said jokingly. A missed period does not automatically mean a woman is pregnant. At the same time, vaginal bleeding does not always indicate a period. Usually, if a menstrual period is one or two days early or late, there is no cause for concern. However, a delay may be a sign of pregnancy. If a woman misses more than two periods in a row or suspects she is pregnant, she should consult a health

When making decisions about an unplanned pregnancy, consider the following questions:

- What are my spiritual and moral beliefs?
- Is raising a child by myself the best choice for the child and me?
- Is raising a child with my partner the best choice for the child and me?
- Is placing the baby for adoption the best choice for the baby and me?
- How would each choice affect my everyday life?
- Which choice could I live with?
- Which choice would be impossible for me?

care professional. Sometimes worrying about the possibility of pregnancy can delay a period.

The physical signs of pregnancy are obvious to some women. They may have a sensitivity to certain aromas, such as coffee, grease, or cigarette smoke. Women may experience nausea and vomiting when they wake up. This is often called "morning sickness." Fatigue and a greater desire to sleep are common complaints. Many women have the need to urinate more frequently. They may crave certain foods. Their breasts are enlarged and tender. As the pregnancy progresses, a woman will notice her abdomen getting larger and feel movement in her belly.

In September of 2003, eighteen-year-old Holly Patterson went to a clinic without her parents' knowledge and took the abortion-drug known as RU-486. She followed the directions and took two more pills at home. The FDA requires patients to return two weeks after taking RU-486 so the physician can confirm a complete termination and the absence of complications. Holly did not go to her follow-up appointment because she was dead. Doctors say Holly died from a massive infection caused by parts of the fetus left inside her uterus that caused her to go into septic shock.

To determine if she is pregnant, a woman can purchase a home pregnancy test at most drugstores. These tests are simple to use, but they may be inaccurate. To be certain if she is pregnant, a woman should have a urine or blood test performed by a health care professional.

An unplanned pregnancy can cause a woman to experience mixed emotions. When she discovers she is pregnant, she may react with fear and disbelief. She may have feelings of guilt and anxiety. Or she may be excited and scared at the same time. She may ask herself: Will I feel well enough to go to school? After the baby is born, will I be able to balance being a mother and going to school or work? What if there is something wrong with the baby?

Once a woman has confirmed she is pregnant, she will need to make some difficult decisions. Every choice will impact the mother, the baby, and other people as well. Sometimes women know immediately what they will do, while others need time to consider their options. The woman may want to sort through her feelings before sharing the results with someone. Although she may feel scared, she needs to exercise courage. Besides seeing a health care provider, the young woman should talk honestly with her parents and the baby's father. A man may not be excited when he first hears the news. He may be worried or afraid. An unplanned pregnancy is difficult for everyone concerned.

After carefully considering her options, a woman may decide to have an abortion to terminate the pregnancy. The word abort means to stop or end something at an early stage. Miscarriage is an abortion that occurs by accident. An induced abortion is a medical procedure done by choice to interrupt an unwanted pregnancy. A doctor or other trained health care professional usually performs an abortion in a clinic or a hospital. Removing the embryo or fetus from the uterus ends the pregnancy.

The abortion pill called RU-486 is a two-drug chemical abortion. The first drug causes the uterine lining to shed, disconnecting the developing unborn child. A second drug is taken a day or two later and causes the womb to expel the now-dead embryo. Taken one after the other, the two drugs cause an induced abortion.

Some family-planning clinics offer counseling, as well as provide abortion services. Abortion may not be an option for some people because of religious or personal values, or because the pregnancy is already too far along. Abortion is a difficult, life-changing decision.

If a woman decides not to terminate the pregnancy, she should begin **prenatal** care as soon as possible—whether she considers adoption or decides to raise the child herself. A medical exam early in the pregnancy will help make sure she is healthy and the pregnancy is

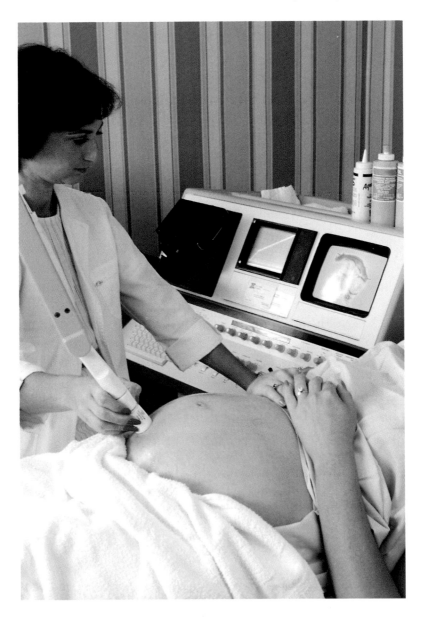

An ultrasound allows medical practitioners to check the baby's development by looking at a visual image on the screen.

Taking Responsibility

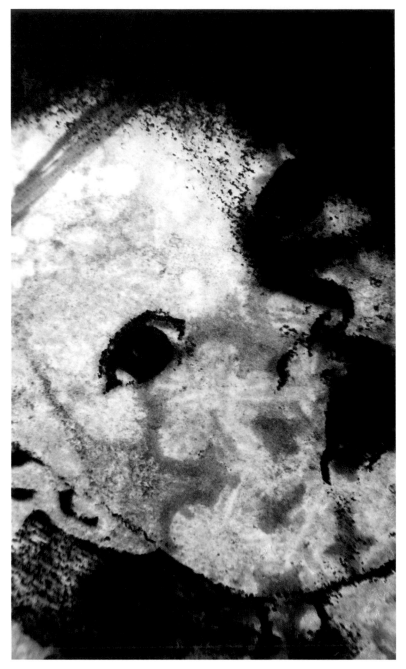

normal. A healthy pregnancy requires some lifestyle changes. She should stop smoking, stop drinking alcohol, and stop using drugs. While the woman is deciding what to do after the baby is born, she must take good care of herself and the developing baby.

Many teen pregnancies are unexpected and at first unwanted, but some are wanted and even planned. Some young women may try to find pleasure and fulfillment by having babies. They view motherhood as a way to become more grown-up and independent. Some teenagers want to escape a difficult home life or want a reason to quit school. Others crave a relationship. These young women want someone to love, who will love them unconditionally in return. Often a woman with low self-esteem doesn't think much of herself or her future. She doesn't have any reason to delay pregnancy. Still others believe pregnancy and children are solutions to boredom, loneliness, or lack of direction. These young women don't have goals, don't like school, and may have grown up in poverty. Often they have grown up without fathers. Sadly, they may think having a child is the best way to keep a boyfriend. Motherhood is viewed as an escape from their difficult circumstances to a more exciting lifestyle. Unfortunately, it rarely turns out that way.

Some men think being able to reproduce proves their manhood and maturity. They may have feared they would not be able to perform. Even though contraceptives usually are easy to obtain, some men don't always use birth control because they think birth control is

> **LATIN LESSON**
>
> The word *pregnant* comes from two Latin words: *prae*, which means before, and *gnas*, which means birth.

inconvenient or interferes with sexual pleasure. Also, men and women think they may be able to choose to have an abortion.

A teenage father certainly has opinions about what his girlfriend should do regarding a pregnancy. In most states, he has no legal right as to whether or not the woman terminates the pregnancy. However, this doesn't mean he should be excluded from discussions. His attitude and support will help the woman make her decision.

Fathers have rights once the baby is born, and with those rights come all the responsibilities of having a family. Sadly, few teenage fathers help maintain their children. Many teenage fathers don't even see their children. Usually a teenage father is out of school, unemployed, and ashamed of his helplessness as a parent. A community program may offer tutoring as well as counseling for teenage fathers. The counselors advise fathers to stay in school or help him find a job if he is ready to work.

A woman's decision whether or not to terminate the pregnancy must be made early in the pregnancy. If she decides not to terminate, she has to decide if she will choose adoption or raise the child. Some teenage girls are convinced adoption is the best choice, while others cannot bear the idea of giving away the baby. (Parenting and adoption are discussed in chapter 8.)

Pregnancy changes lives. Giving up a baby for adoption is difficult. Being a single parent is difficult. Being a single teen parent is even more difficult. Some teenagers are fortunate enough to be able to live with their parents who will help raise the child. Other teens are less fortunate and are forced to find other living arrangements. A teenager may receive a lot of advice about her pregnancy. She may even feel pressured into doing something that someone else thinks is right. In the end, the young woman will have to live with her decision the rest of her life.

5

FIRST TRIMESTER

Mr. Mitchell's students listened intently as the nurse practitioner explained the models and charts showing a woman's body through all stages of pregnancy. The students started to whisper as they watched the slide presentation *Preview of a Birth*.

"It has a heartbeat already?" Shawna's voice climbed above the students' whispers.

"Yes, it does," the nurse practitioner said. Her straightforward approach encouraged the students to ask questions, one after another.

"Can it breathe?"

"Can you tell if it's a boy or a girl?"

"How early are abortions performed?"

"Can the baby feel it?"

The nurse practitioner answered every question, explaining the medical facts. The students absorbed the information like sponges. The bell rang, and Shawna walked out of the classroom with her hand on her abdomen.

At the **obstetrician**'s office, the nurse told Logan to stay in the waiting room while Shawna followed the nurse to an examining room. She recorded Shawna's height and weight, and then checked Shawna's vital signs (temperature, blood pressure, and pulse).

"The bathroom is on the other side of this door," the nurse said. "Please leave a urine sample in the paper cup on the back of the toilet. You will need to get completely undressed and put on this gown with the opening in the back. Dr. Jones will be with you soon." The nurse closed the door on her way out.

Dr. Jones knocked on the door and entered the examining room. He introduced himself and shook Shawna's hand. They talked for a few minutes, and then he left the room and returned with the nurse.

After Dr. Jones completed Shawna's physical exam, Logan was asked to join Shawna. Dr. Jones performed an ultrasound, and he said both Shawna and the fetus appeared healthy. Using the date of Shawna's last menstrual period, along with the measurements recorded during the ultrasound, Dr. Jones determined an expected due date. He told Shawna she should not drink alcohol or smoke cigarettes, to eat healthy, to get plenty of rest, and to call if she had any problems. He would see her once a month for the next several months. The nurse gave Shawna information on what to expect during pregnancy, and the nurse handed Logan a brochure for expectant fathers.

"Shawna, Young Moms is a program designed for young mothers like yourself. You meet once a week with other moms, and a trained facilitator will lead group discussions on various topics. Also, you will be assigned a caseworker who will help you learn about community services and agencies," the nurse said.

Taking Responsibility

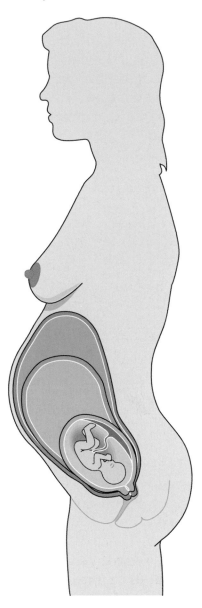

By the end of the first trimester (the first three months of pregnancy) the baby and uterus are about this big. By the end of nine months, the uterus will have grown to the size of the larger outline.

LATIN LESSON

Fetus comes from the Latin word meaning "young one" or "offspring."

The word *umbilicus* means "navel," and *navel* is another word for "belly button."

Shawna asked the nurse to schedule an appointment with Young Moms. After the nurse left the room, Shawna changed into her clothes.

"What are you going to do?" Logan asked. "I'm going to the university this fall. I can't lose my scholarship."

"Logan, didn't you watch the monitor during the ultrasound? We are having *a baby*! Do what you have to do; go to college. But I will not end the pregnancy—whether or not you're with me."

Later that week, a caseworker from Young Moms took Shawna to the Department of Social Services. The caseworker helped Shawna complete paperwork to get Medicaid.

"You also need to start thinking about raising the baby yourself or adoption. No matter what you choose, your decision will impact more people than just you and the baby," the caseworker said.

"How will I know what is best?" Shawna asked.

"Try and imagine the baby's life—not just as a newborn, but throughout the entire childhood. You have already made difficult decisions. You can make more."

Gestation is the time between conception and the birth of the baby, when the baby is growing inside the mother's

Healthy Hints

- Eat good foods (fruits, vegetables, cereals, breads, rice, beans, dairy products, fish, meat, and poultry).
- Drink eight glasses of water every day.
- Stay active and get regular exercise.
- Get plenty of sleep.
- Do not eat junk food.
- Do not drink alcohol or drinks with caffeine, such as coffee or soda.
- Do not smoke.
- Do not take any drugs or medications—even aspirin—without checking with your health care provider.

womb. In human beings, pregnancy or gestation averages 266 days or forty weeks. This is 280 days or about nine months from the beginning of the last menstrual period. The gestation period is divided into three trimesters. Each trimester is three months.

The baby grows in the uterus—not in the stomach. By attaching to the wall of the uterus, the developing baby is able to receive nutrition from the mother's glands and blood vessels within the uterine lining. In the uterus, a sac filled with a watery fluid forms around the developing baby and protects it against pokes, bumps, and jolts. The sac is called the amniotic sac or the "bag of waters," and the fluid is called amniotic fluid. This fluid is warm and keeps the developing baby warm as it floats. As the developing baby grows bigger, the uterus grows bigger. Early in pregnancy, a structure forms in the uterus that enables the embryo to receive the food, water, and oxygen it needs. This is called the **placenta**.

The umbilical cord is a rope-like cord that connects the placenta to the fetus. The placenta supplies the fetus with oxygen from the air the mother breathes and nutrients from the food she eats. Oxygen and nutrients pass from the placenta to the fetus in the blood that flows through the umbilical cord. Waste from the fetus leaves the mother's body along with the mother's waste.

Medicines, drugs, and alcohol can also pass into the developing baby's blood from the mother's blood. That's why a pregnant female should be very careful about what she eats, drinks, and puts into her body. If she needs to take a prescription drug, she should check with her health care provider to make sure the drug will not hurt the fetus.

If a female has smoked cigarettes, consumed alcohol, taken drugs, or had certain infections while pregnant, her baby could be born with or develop serious health problems. The baby could have difficulty eating, breathing, and growing properly. If a pregnant woman has been addicted to drugs, her baby may be born addicted to drugs. However, if the woman has regular checkups with a health care provider, eats healthy foods, exercises regularly, and gets enough sleep, her baby will have the best chance to be born healthy.

Going to the Doctor

A pregnant woman's first prenatal visit will include a complete physical exam and review of her medical history. The health care provider will check the woman's

A multiple birth is when two or more babies are born at the same birth. Identical twins begin when a fertilized cell implants itself and divides into two separate parts. Each embryo then develops independently. Identical twins are always the same sex and usually look almost exactly like each other.

Fraternal twins begin when separate sperm fertilize two eggs at about the same time. Each fallopian tube contains an egg, or one tube contains two eggs. When the sperm cells enter the tubes, both eggs are fertilized. Each egg becomes separately implanted in the uterus, and each embryo has a placenta. Fraternal twins can be the same gender or opposite sexes. They are ordinary brothers or sisters whose original egg cells just happened to be fertilized at the same time and who were therefore born at the same time.

Triplets, quadruplets, and quintuplets are much rarer and are usually products of two or more eggs. Triplets most commonly result from two eggs, one of which divides to produce a pair of identical twins while the other egg produces a single infant.

vital signs and listen to the woman's heart and lungs. The woman needs to get used to being weighed because it happens at each appointment during a pregnancy. A mother's weight is one tool to help determine if the baby is developing properly. The woman should gain approximately two pounds a month. The health care provider will also determine the woman's due date if it has not yet been decided.

A gynecologic exam is also called a pelvic exam, vaginal exam, or internal exam. During this exam, the woman lies on her back on the examining table. She places her feet in metal stirrups and is asked to keep her knees apart. The health care provider checks the external genital organs. Then using a *speculum*, the health care provider views the cervix. Also, the health care provider gently examines the size and position of the uterus, the fallopian tubes, and the ovaries. The health care provider may perform a rectal exam, feeling inside the anus and rectum for lumps, swelling, or obstruction. The gynecologic exam includes checking a woman's breasts for lumps. The health care provider should explain everything that takes place during the exam. However, many

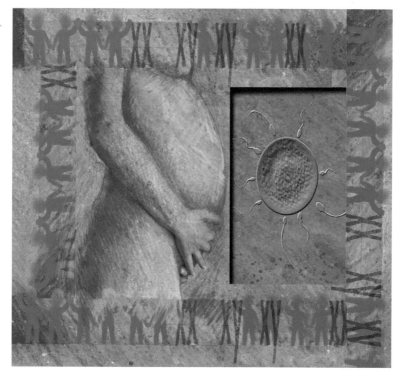

women are nervous during a gynecologic exam. To relax, a woman can take slow, deep breaths. Talking, asking questions, or sharing concerns with the health care provider during the exam may also help ease emotional tension.

At the earliest time a pregnancy is determined, the fetus will already be four or six weeks' gestation. If there are no problems, the teen mother should be able to continue attending school. She will be tired because her body is producing more blood. She may also feel nauseated or sick to her stomach. Some women are sick every morning and at other times during the day. Eating a few saltine crackers before getting out of bed in the morning will help. The mother may have to urinate frequently. During this first trimester, the mother's breasts may feel tender and heavy as milk glands begin to grow.

The First Trimester

The first trimester is the first twelve weeks of pregnancy. During this trimester, a pregnant woman's body changes significantly. A sperm joins an ovum to form one cell during Week One. This **zygote** is smaller than a grain of salt. Once this happens, the developing human is called an embryo. During Week Two, the fertilized egg implants itself in the lining of the uterus and begins to take nourishment. A woman is still unaware of her pregnancy during Week Three, but she is about to miss her first menstrual period. At one month old (Week Four), the embryo is ten thousand times larger than the original fertilized egg. The backbone and muscles are forming. Arms, legs, eyes, and ears have begun to show.

> ### Ectopic Pregnancy
>
> An ectopic pregnancy is when a fertilized egg begins developing outside the uterus, most often inside a woman's fallopian tube. This is a serious medical condition, because the fallopian tube may rupture. This type of pregnancy is also called a tubal pregnancy.

During Week Five, the developing baby's leg and arm buds are now clearly visible. Week Six is when the mother is about to miss her second period and has probably confirmed she is pregnant. The embryo's brain begins to control movement of muscles and organs. At Week Seven, the embryo begins to move spontaneously. Teeth buds form in the gums.

Week Eight is when the developing baby is called a fetus. Although the mother will not be able to feel movement until the fourth or fifth month, the fetus responds to touch. Fingerprints are evidenced in the skin during Week Nine, and internal organs are present and functioning. Changes after this week are primarily in size, rather than in appearance.

The uterus has doubled in size by Week Ten. The fetus can squint, swallow, and wrinkle its forehead. At Week Eleven, the fetus is about two inches long, and the face has a baby's profile. The fetus sleeps, awakens, and exercises its muscles at Week Twelve. The first trimester closes at the end of the third month.

6

Second and Third Trimesters

During the second trimester, Shawna felt like she had before becoming pregnant. The nausea had disappeared, and she no longer napped after school. Spring had arrived, so she walked outside thirty minutes every day. As the weeks progressed, her excitement grew, her body grew, and the tension in her home grew.

The caseworker from Young Moms helped Shawna access community resources and services. Even though Tori listened and offered suggestions, Shawna needed someone older who had experience in guiding people in how to handle stress. Through a program called Smart Choices, every week a mentor from the women's health clinic met with Shawna. The mentor helped Shawna set realistic goals and develop important life skills.

Whenever Shawna was home, she tried to ignore Bill's comments about "getting knocked up." Although Shawna spoke to her mother about Bill, the stress at home became unbearable.

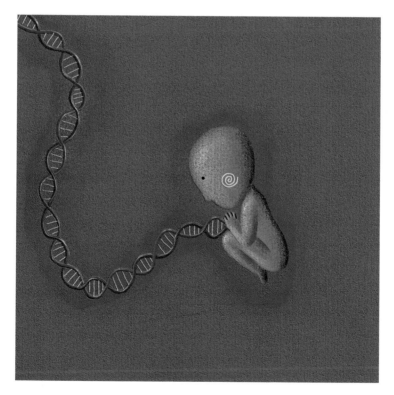

"I can't take this anymore. I have to find somewhere else to live. I thought about asking to live with my grandmother, but she lives in another school district. I've even heard about families helping in situations like this, but I don't know anyone who would want me," Shawna said.

"There is another option," the mentor said. "Liberty House is a transitional home for women and their young children in need of care, shelter, and protection. Just today I learned there is an available room because a young woman has decided to move out. She's going to stay with a family from her church. If you'd like, I can make an appointment for you to visit the home."

"Yes, please," Shawna said.

The following weekend, Shawna moved to Liberty House. The large home accommodated up to ten women and their children. One woman had recently been released from prison and wanted to learn to live free from drugs and crimes. Several women were from abusive homes. One teenager had a young son and was pregnant with her second baby. Each woman had her own bedroom and shared a bathroom connecting to another bedroom. All ten women shared housekeeping and cooking responsibilities. A housemother lived with the women, supervising the residents and maintaining order in the house. Liberty House was near the bus route, so Shawna could easily get to school and her appointments. She could not depend on Logan or her mother anymore. Moving out of her house was easier than Shawna expected.

Tori and Shawna talked every day at school. Tori always listened as Shawna complained about her changing body, especially the stretch marks and how she felt as big as a whale. Tori tried to assure Shawna that she looked beautiful, and she would fit in her jeans after the baby was born.

"I'm writing in my journal almost every day. I write about my feelings and what's happening with the pregnancy. Next week I'm checking out a day care center for moms who want to finish school. I also have an appointment with an adoption agency. I have to seriously think about what I'm going to do about the baby. I can't put off the decision much longer. So what are you writing about these days?" Shawna asked.

"I mostly write about Carlos. I'm trying to go slow because I don't want to mess up this relationship," Tori said.

"I was never good at that." Shawna rubbed her large belly.

"Carlos is different. He's a gentleman."

"Be careful, Tori, or you may end up like me," Shawna said.

The Second Trimester

For many women, the second trimester is the most comfortable time of pregnancy. Women at this stage of pregnancy often feel better and are not concerned yet about the third trimester delivery. During this trimester, the woman's uterus grows significantly as the baby undergoes a tremendous growth spurt. Not only does the woman's outward appearance change, her body continues making internal changes. She may not feel sick to her stomach, and food will even start to smell good again. The woman will have increased energy. As a result of the presence or increase in hormones, her hair may become

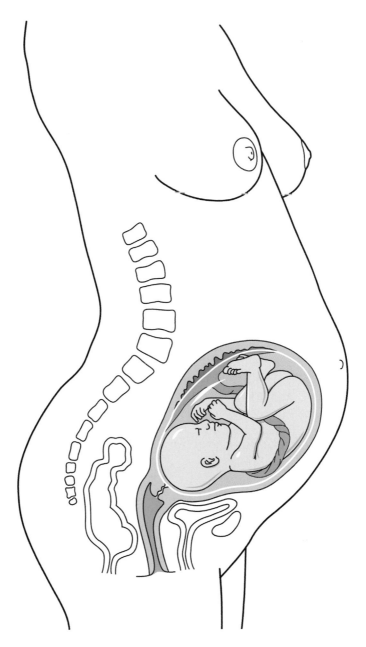

Development by the end of the second trimester.

thicker and more luxurious than usual. The extra hair growth is temporary and most will disappear after birth.

However, this stage of pregnancy also has its discomforts. A woman's growing uterus creates upward pressure on her organs. The uterus is entirely separate from the stomach. As the uterus expands, it presses on the bladder and stomach and all the other organs. This explains why the mother needs to urinate more often than usual, and she needs to eat smaller, more frequent meals. Her body needs extra fluid, so she should drink approximately eight to ten cups a day. The pressure of her growing uterus on her bowels may interfere with elimination and increase the likelihood of constipation. She should take in lots of fluid and fiber in her diet, and moderate exercise if permitted by her health care provider. She may also experience heartburn and indigestion.

Backaches may become worse as the size of her belly increases and her center of gravity shifts forward. She should not wear high heels. Some women develop varicose veins. A woman can prevent or minimize varicose veins by avoiding pressure on the veins by walking twenty minutes every day to exercise and improve circulation and muscle tone in her legs. Muscle cramps often occur at night. She can ask her health care provider about taking calcium and potassium supplements.

Dizziness is often caused by a sudden change in position. To prevent dizziness, she should move her legs when sitting, stand up gradually, and put one hand on something for support if she feels lightheaded. She may also have more headaches. If she experiences severe headaches and cannot find relief, she should call her health care provider. She should always consult her health care provider before taking any medications. Stretch marks occur when the skin is stretched beyond its capacity and it tears. When the skin covering a preg-

To avoid heartburn and indigestion:

- Eat several small meals throughout the day instead of three big ones.
- Eat slowly, chewing food carefully and completely.
- Eat boiled or broiled food. Do not eat fried, spicy, or fatty foods.
- Do not drink coffee, soda, or alcohol.
- Avoid clothing that puts pressure on the stomach (tight waistbands or belts).

nant woman's abdomen is stretched, the skin can become itchy. Frequent massages with moisturizing cream will help decrease itchiness.

She will see her health care provider approximately every four weeks during the second trimester. In addition to checking the woman's vital signs and weight, the health care provider will measure the size of the uterus and listen to the fetal heartbeat. The woman may have additional tests ordered. She should discuss with her health care provider any concerns she has about changes or discomforts.

At the beginning of the second trimester, the baby is completely formed. At four months, its bones have begun to develop, and its arms and legs can move. The mother may now experience *quickening*. One way of describing the first

When the mother smokes, the heartbeat of the fetus speeds up. Mothers who smoke cigarettes tend to have smaller babies and more complications than mothers who do not smoke.

Taking Responsibility

Photographs taken of an unborn child within the womb.

kicks is a feeling like little bubbles or a fluttering in the stomach. Feeling the baby move for the first time makes the pregnancy concrete for many women and their partners. Like many expectant mothers, she may begin to talk to the baby and may use a nickname

> To relieve headache pain, place an ice pack at the back of the mother's neck or on top of her head. Also, fresh air, an hour or two in a quiet dark room, or a nap may lessen the pain.

for the baby. At five months, the fetus would be about ten inches long if its legs were stretched out straight, and it weighs about three-quarters of a pound. At six months, the fetus is beginning to look a lot like a human baby, except it is thin and has not yet begun to store up fat. At the end of the second trimester, the baby will be able to move its limbs, make a fist, suck its thumb, and even hiccup.

Fetal Alcohol Syndrome

If the mother drinks alcohol, the baby's movements inside the uterus slow down while the alcohol is in the mother's bloodstream. Some babies of alcoholic mothers are born with a disorder called fetal alcohol syndrome. This disorder is the third leading cause of birth defects in the United States. It causes physical deformities and mental retardation. Heavy drinking by a pregnant woman is very harmful to the baby, both at birth and through its life.

The Third Trimester

The third trimester is a time for excitement and anxiety. Now the mother feels the baby kicking. Sometimes the mother can even make out the shape of her baby's foot or rear end pressing against the skin of her abdomen. The mother's emotions will run high. She will become more nervous as the due date gets closer. Fear of the birth process, worries about new responsibilities, and finances are added stresses for the mother (and father if he is involved). The woman should try to enjoy this time. Often, women play music for the baby. Some women talk or sing to their unborn babies.

Unborn twins.

Drugs, especially heroin, are harmful to the baby. As the mother becomes addicted to heroin, the baby also becomes addicted. After the baby is born, the baby goes through painful and serious withdrawal symptoms, just as an adult does when taken off the drug.

Although the mother is pleased to know the baby will soon be here, the final three months are physically less comfortable for her. The baby grows rapidly and becomes heavier. As her body's center of gravity changes, she is more likely to have accidents on stairs and uneven ground, like gravel or broken sidewalks. Her thirst will increase. The mother's hands, ankles, and feet may swell. She may have to buy larger shoes. She should consider removing her rings before swelling reaches the point where she cannot remove them. She should elevate her feet for about an hour each day, avoid sitting for lengthy periods of time, and move around so that circulation increases.

Because the uterus presses down on her bladder, pregnancy *incontinence* may occur when a woman coughs, sneezes, or laughs. To avoid leaking, the woman needs to keep her bladder as empty as possible by urinating frequently. She can also wear a panty

Why use an ultrasound?

- to check the fetus.
- to verify the due date.
- to measure different parts of the fetus.
- to verify the location of the placenta.
- to check for multiple fetuses.
- to evaluate the amount of amniotic fluid.

liner or a sanitary pad, but should change it frequently. A pregnant woman may develop hemorrhoids. These are varicose or swollen rectal veins that are either internal or bulge out of the anus. They are caused when a pregnant woman is constipated and strains to eliminate hard stools. Hemorrhoids may itch and become irritated. They may also bleed, especially after a bowel movement. She can apply ice compresses or ask her health care provider to recommend a medicated ointment or pad that will help soothe the area. In addition to moderate exercise, drinking lots of fluids and increasing the fiber content of her diet, the woman's health care provider can also suggest a stool softener or a fiber supplement.

A woman's heart needs to work harder to improve circulation through the uterus and the placenta. She may begin to feel short of breath. If this happens, she should

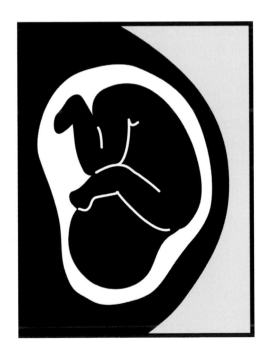

slow down or take a break if she is in the middle of an activity. Regular exercise improves the efficiency of her respiratory system, circulation, and muscle tone; but she should continue exercising at a slower pace. Changing her position will

> Swimming is a relaxing and effective form of exercise. The water helps support the mother's extra weight and minimizes stress on her joints.

help. If it is harder to breathe when lying down, she can prop herself with pillows or sleep in a reclining chair. Some women experience more dreams during pregnancy, while others find it difficult to get a good night's sleep. Napping during the day may help.

Pregnant women experience gentle contractions called Braxton-Hicks contractions. These last usually less than one minute and are painless. She will feel as if her uterus is gradually becoming tight and then relaxing. These contractions may be called false labor because they don't lead to childbirth, but sometimes an expectant mother thinks she is about to give birth. She can consider these as practice contractions that help her uterus prepare for the actual delivery.

Visits to her health care provider will be scheduled every other week during the last trimester. Then in the last month, she will see her health care provider each week until she gives birth. In the ninth month of pregnancy, a woman may stop gaining weight or even lose weight. A few weeks before going into labor, some women feel energetic and elated. Routine procedures will be the same as in the second trimester. Also, she will be checked for diabetes. If a woman has diabetes, she will be placed on a low-sugar diet and will be tested regularly for blood sugar level. The pregnancy should be closely monitored, especially as the due date approaches.

> The technician and health care provider may be able to tell if the baby is a boy or a girl. However, sometimes the baby's legs may block the view. If a woman wants to know her baby's gender, she should ask the technician. Some people prefer the surprise of not finding out until the baby is born.

If a woman ever notices a sudden decrease in her baby's movement or if the baby doesn't move at all, the mother should call her health care provider. This doesn't necessarily mean there are problems, but tests will be taken to assess the baby's well-being. Although problems still occur, the health care provider can remedy most of them so the mother and baby come through the delivery fine. Encountering a problem during pregnancy or childbirth is always emotionally difficult. However, people grow stronger no matter the outcome.

Each day during the third trimester, the baby will grow stronger. At seven months, it is fourteen inches long and probably weighs over two pounds. The baby is considered viable by the twenty-fourth week and later. This means if the baby is born this early, the baby could survive with proper medical attention in an intensive-care nursery. Such a baby is called ***premature***, since it is born before the full term of nine months. A premature baby may be born with several problems. Neonatal intensive care units and the use of drugs before and after delivery help more babies survive premature delivery.

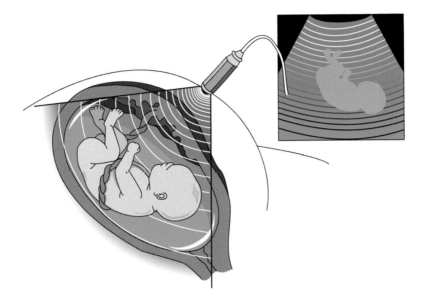

An ultrasound uses sound waves to create an image of the unborn fetus.

During months eight and nine, the fetus grows to an average weight of seven or eight pounds. By the beginning of the ninth month, the baby will have long nails on its toes and fingers. At the end of the forty weeks, the baby is ready to be born.

7
LABOR AND DELIVERY

Shawna woke up and noticed her bed sheets were wet. She called Tori.

"I need you. I think I am in labor," Shawna said.
As soon as Shawna arrived at the Labor and Delivery

unit, she was taken into a birthing room and given a hospital gown. A few minutes later, a resident doctor examined her.

"Your water has broken, so you'll be delivering your baby within twenty-four hours," the resident said.

"But I'm two days early! Does that mean the baby is a preemie?" Shawna asked.

"No, the baby is not premature. Your due date is an estimate. No one really knows when a woman will deliver her baby, unless she's scheduled for a **cesarean section** or her labor is **induced**. We will monitor the baby during your labor. You have taken good care of yourself throughout your pregnancy, so your baby should be fine. I'll call Dr. Jones. He will be here closer to the time of delivery. I want you to rest now." The resident left the room.

"How are you feeling?" Tori asked.

"Not too bad. The contractions feel like I'm having a period," Shawna said.

"Let me know when you feel a lot of discomfort. The doctor has ordered some medicine for that," the nurse said. "Is there anything else I can do for you right now?"

"I am hungry. I didn't eat breakfast," Shawna said.

"No eating. Sorry, but that is a rule for all patients in labor. Your stomach needs to be empty in case you have general anesthesia. I'll bring you some ice chips," the nurse said.

Labor progressed at a steady pace without complications. Tori helped Shawna relax by taking deep breaths. Later, an **anesthesiologist** administered an **epidural**. The nurse hooked up a fetal monitor to check the baby's heart rate, and frequently took Shawna's vital signs. When Shawna's cervix was fully dilated, the nurse paged Dr. Jones. A few minutes later, he came into Shawna's room wearing a mask, a gown, and gloves.

Taking Responsibility

"When I tell you, I want you to bear down and out, just as if you were pushing out a bowel movement," Dr. Jones said. "Don't worry about pushing out stool. If stool comes out, the nurse will wipe it away with one of the disposable liners under you. We are used to these sorts of things, so don't be nervous."

Apgar score is a test developed by Virginia Apgar, a New York anesthesiologist. The heart rate, muscle tone, respiration, reflexes, and color are assessed one minute after birth and five minutes after birth. Each vital sign is given a score of zero, one, or two. A high Apgar usually means the baby is healthy and does not need further assistance. A low score indicates that the baby needs some immediate attention; for example, the baby might need extra breathing support.

"I don't want to rip," Shawna said.

"I don't want you to either. Do you remember we discussed an **episiotomy**? This will make space for the baby to pass through." Dr. Jones numbed Shawna and made a small incision.

"Look!" Tori said. She pointed to a large mirror at the end of the bed. "You can see the baby's head."

"This is called crowning. It is the first sign of the actual birth. We have this large mirror here so you can see the baby's head as you push," Dr. Jones said. "It shouldn't be long now. The time between crowning and actual delivery is usually very short."

Shawna wanted to watch, but she closed her eyes to concentrate on pushing. A few minutes later, the doctor suctioned the baby's mouth and nose, cut the umbilical cord, and held up the baby. The baby cried.

94

"You have a baby girl," Dr. Jones said.

Shawna cried.

"Why are you crying?" Tori asked.

"I'm so happy," Shawna said. "A girl! I have a daughter."

After the baby's Apgar score was recorded, a nurse wrapped the baby in a blanket and placed her on Shawna's chest. Tori took pictures.

"I'll bathe the baby and bring her back in a few minutes," a nurse said.

"We have a little more work to do," Dr. Jones said.

After Shawna delivered the placenta, the doctor stitched the episiotomy incision. A nurse washed Shawna and helped her change into a fresh gown. A few minutes later, another nurse returned with the baby.

"Does she have ten fingers and ten toes?" Shawna asked.

"Yes. She looks just like you," Tori said. "She's perfect."

Labor

Most pregnant women ask, "How will I know when it's time to deliver?" Chances are labor will not begin on a woman's actual due date. Contractions may begin as twinges that won't interrupt what a woman is doing and eventually reach a point where she can no longer talk through them. A woman's labor may begin with mild contractions that slowly build up over hours, or it may begin with regular and intense contractions. For some women, labor begins after the water has broken.

Labor can be as short as an hour or longer than a day. Labor goes through three stages. During the first stage, contractions cause the cervix to efface (thin) and dilate (open). When the cervix is fully dilated to about ten cen-

Taking Responsibility

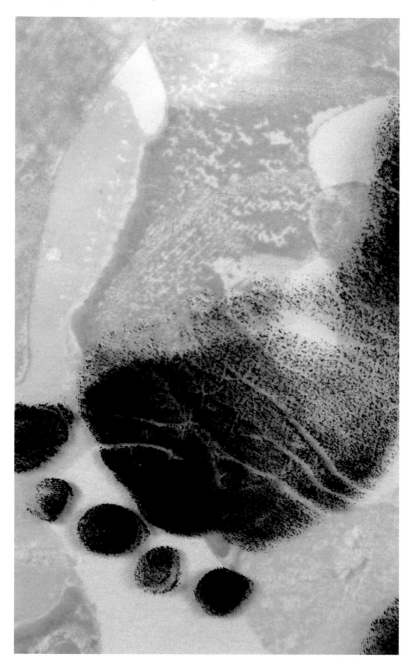

timeters, a woman is ready to push. The second stage begins at this point and ends when the baby is born. The length of this stage depends on many factors, including the size of the baby and if the mother has had previous vaginal deliveries. The second stage is when women do their most work. The third stage lasts from the moment

Each labor is different. Generally, labor lasts longer for first-time mothers than for women who have already given birth. It could take twenty-four hours or only four hours. Once labor starts, a woman should not make any plans for at least forty-eight hours.

the baby is born until the placenta is separated from the wall of the uterus and expelled from the vagina.

A woman's cervix can be fully effaced and a couple of centimeters dilated for a few days or even a couple weeks before she goes into labor. Several other signs indicate when a woman's body is getting ready to go into labor. Engagement refers to the baby's descent into the pelvis. It is also called dropping or lightening. As the baby descends, the mother will find it easier to breathe because the baby is no longer pressing against her diaphragm and lungs. But because the baby is lower, the mother will feel increased pressure on her bowel and bladder, causing constipation and frequent urination. Amniotic fluid should look similar to urine—clear or light yellow. Sometimes it is lightly tinged with blood. A pink-colored or blood-streaked vaginal discharge may appear. This is called the "mucus plug," which usually seals the cervix and becomes loose when the cervix dilates.

Throughout labor, the mother's vital signs will be checked regularly, as well as the dilation of her cervix. If the mother's health care provider is not already at the

Taking Responsibility

> The baby's heart rate is monitored during labor. This can be done by attaching a monitor to the mother's abdomen or internally with a monitor. The monitor records the fetal heart rate and uterine contractions, and then records the results as a graph. Monitoring the fetus allows the health care provider to track the baby's health.

hospital, the staff will take the mother's vital signs, listen to the fetal heartbeat, and examine the mother to decide whether or not she should be admitted. The mother may have an intravenous line started. This will give her health care provider immediate access to the mother's system in case medication is needed.

Pain has always been associated with childbirth. Mothers can now choose to practice natural pain relief techniques or accept medication. The techniques learned in childbirth classes—breathing, focus exercises, and massages—help reduce the pain of childbirth for many women. Narcotics are sometimes used for pain relief in labor. Usually these drugs are injected either through an intravenous line or in the arm or hip. They are used to dull the pain of contractions.

Before a woman is admitted to the hospital, she and her health care provider should discuss the types of anesthetic. One anesthetic commonly used during labor is the *epidural*. Spinal anesthesia or general anesthesia may be used for a cesarean section.

Labor is another word for work. Courses are available to help the mother understand labor and delivery. The mother should communicate her needs and feelings so her health care provider and nurses can help her have a good experience of childbirth.

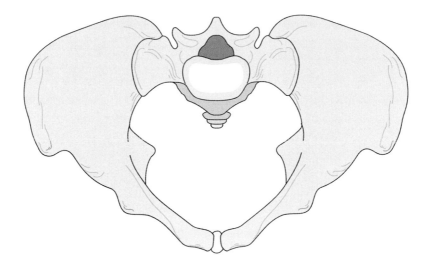

Usually, the larger a woman's pelvic structure, the more easily the baby can be delivered.

During the birth, the baby travels out of the uterus, through the cervix, and into the vagina. The vagina stretches as the baby travels through it and out of the mother's body. The vagina is often called the birth canal because canal is another word for passageway. When it is time to push, squatting or standing can sometimes help the mother push with the aid of gravity. The mother does not have to push continuously. If she has had a baby before, or if the baby is small, the time needed for pushing

The labor coach:

- helps the mother maintain proper breathing techniques.
- offers emotional support.
- massages various parts of the mother's body.
- makes sure the mother is as comfortable as possible.
- holds and coaches the mother while she pushes.

may be very short. If this is her first baby or if this baby is bigger than her other babies, it will probably take longer.

The health care provider may perform an episiotomy. This procedure takes place just before the baby's head crowns to make space for the baby to pass through. The first glimpse of the baby gives most mothers a final burst of strength to finish the delivery. Most of the time, the baby's head comes out first. A baby may arrive face up, but it is usually face down. Before delivering the rest of the baby's body, the health care provider will make sure the umbilical cord is not wrapped around the baby's neck, then suction the baby's nose and mouth, and wipe the baby's face. The baby's head will turn, and the rest of the baby is delivered. A clamp will be placed in each of two sections of the umbilical cord, and then the cord is cut between the two clamps. If the mother or coach want to help cut the umbilical cord, the mother should tell the health care provider to let her know when it is the right time.

Sometimes the health care provider uses ***forceps*** or a ***vacuum*** to help ease the baby out of the vaginal canal.

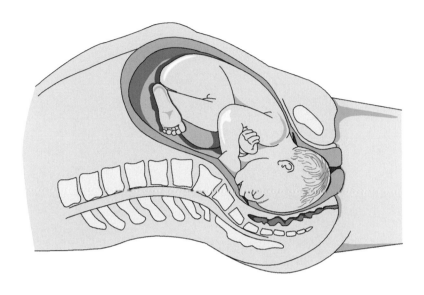

Stages of delivery.

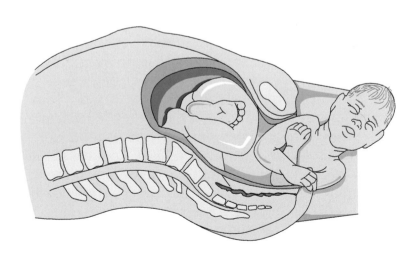

These instruments are used when the baby's head is already in the vagina. This type of help is necessary when the mother is exhausted from pushing, or there is a need to speed up the delivery of the baby, or when a cesarean section is not immediately available.

After the umbilical cord is cut, the newborn is handed to a nurse or **pediatrician**, or placed on the mother's abdomen or in a crib. Babies do not have to scream loudly to be healthy. The baby's status is checked and rated. A few minutes after the baby is born, the placenta or afterbirth is delivered. If the baby is in good health, the mother will be given some time to spend with the baby right after birth. The mother may try to breast-feed, but some babies learn about breast-feeding along with the mother.

The moment has arrived when a mother and/or father can finally hold the newborn. Some parents will hold the baby as soon as it's born, while other mothers need time to rest first. But sometime soon, the mother and/or father will begin holding, feeding, and touching the baby. And the baby will respond to voices, smells, and touch.

Did you know?

- Miscarriages and *stillbirths* are more frequent among teens than among adult women.
- Teens under the age of fifteen have high rates of pregnancy complications.
- Teens are twice as likely to have premature infants.

Bonding has begun. For many women, labor and delivery are painful. For most women, this life-changing event is worth all the hard work.

B

PARENTING OR ADOPTION

"I told Carlos about my past," Tori said.

"What did he say?" Shawna asked.

"He told me he still loves me, and he agreed to honor my decision to practice secondary virginity."

Taking Responsibility

Shawna smiled. "I'm so happy for you."

"Have you heard from Logan since you came home from the hospital?" Tori asked.

"He did visit me at the hospital, but he told me to give up the baby for adoption."

"Are you seriously considering not keeping the baby?"

"When I visited the adoption agency last month, I looked through a book with information and photographs of all those families wanting to adopt a baby. Some of those people could give her a beautiful home and things. But I know that if I choose adoption, it may be out of pity for one of those couples. That is not the right reason to give up my baby. I don't know if I can raise her by myself. I'm exhausted. I don't know what I would do if you weren't staying with me this first week home. Thanks for changing all those diapers! Now that I can pump my breast milk, you can feed the baby so I can get some more sleep.

"I'm glad to help. I enjoy holding her."

"But you have your own life. You have school, your job, and Carlos."

"Have you talked with your mom?"

"Mom loves me, but I'm not sure how much she will help me. She reminds me she will not raise my baby. Anyway, I will not live in the same house with Bill. I need a peaceful home," Shawna said. "I just don't know if I can do this by myself."

"Try to not worry. People will help." Tori hugged her best friend.

Shawna visited Mom's House. The day care was in a building attached to a church. Years before, the building had been used as a school, but now several community agencies occupied the space. The second floor was designated for Mom's House. In addition to a kitchen and

Babies have many needs. Sometimes the most responsible decision is to choose to turn all those responsibilities over to people who are at a point in their lives where they can more easily meet those many needs. When that's the case, adoption can be an act of love on the part of everyone involved.

Taking Responsibility

bathrooms, the children were supervised in one of four rooms. A child was assigned to a room according to the child's age: infants, older babies, two-year-olds, or three- and four-year-olds. Shawna noticed that the rooms were decorated in bright colors, and each room had a cross hanging on a wall. The rooms also held age-appropriate toys and furniture.

The director explained the day care program followed government regulations for staffing and meals. The children were provided breakfast, lunch, and an afternoon snack. This particular day care was offered only to single parents who attended school full time. In exchange for free day care services, the parent agrees to attend school regularly, maintain passing grades, give three hours of service to the center each week, and complete five hours of fundraising each semester.

"This may be an answer to prayer." Shawna completed an application.

"Tori, I actually fit in my jeans again!" Shawna looked in the mirror. "Logan came over yesterday. He even held the baby for a few minutes. He agreed to pay child support. It won't be much money because he's working part time and going to college, but at least he's accepting some responsibility as a father. I hope he sees his daughter more than my father sees me."

"People can change," Tori said.

"Time will tell. Did I mention I've been approved to continue living at Liberty House this year? And now that the baby is old enough, she has been accepted at Mom's House, so I can go to school." Shawna kissed her baby's forehead. "Being a single parent is difficult, but I know we are safe and healthy. And although it's just the two of us, my baby and I are a real family."

Making up your mind whether to parent or put your child up for adoption is a serious and difficult decision.

Taking Responsibility

Babies quickly learn the way to get what they need is to cry. But many babies cry a lot during the first month, whether they need something or not. Holding and cuddling is very important for babies. Being held close while feeding provides the feeling of warmth and closeness that the baby needs. A baby's feeding time is also pleasant and healthy for the mother. A newborn has very strong sucking muscles and a little pad of fat in each cheek to help it. The baby will suck on anything that is put near its mouth.

A new mother should call her health care provider if she has problems before her six-week checkup. Problems such as:

- signs of an infection.
- vaginal discharge that becomes bright red or is foul smelling.
- severe and persistent abdominal pain.
- persistent fever.
- any other unusual problems.

The first day or two after birth, the mother's breasts produce a liquid called colostrum. This yellowish substance provides both nourishment and antibodies that help protect the baby from infections. When the baby is ready for more, the mother's breasts will become hard and engorged with milk. Even if a new mother does not breast-feed, her breasts will become filled with milk. If she does not nurse the baby, the milk production will stop by itself within a few weeks.

Breast-feeding (also called nursing) is a learning experience for both mother and baby. Sometimes babies find it difficult at first to put their mouths around the nipple correctly. Many medical facilities have *lactation* experts, who are trained to help new mothers and their babies succeed at breast-feeding.

Bottle-feeding is a perfectly safe and healthy way to feed the baby for mothers who cannot or choose not to breast-feed. Many good mothers do not wish or are unable to nurse their babies. These babies are fed from a bottle that contains a special formula similar to breast milk, and they can grow to be strong and healthy.

When a mother and her baby are home from the hospital, the mother will discover the joy of parenthood can also be a time of adjustment and exhaustion. Sometimes newborns have their days and nights confused. Mothers may have to adapt as best as they can by sleeping when the baby sleeps. Rest is the key to good health and the ability to be a good parent.

The mother needs to recover physically. She will feel all types of emotions, and the baby will make constant demands. A new mother may find herself overwhelmed with all the chores that need to be done when she is by herself. Some mothers have a relative stay and help for the first few days. How much time a mother needs to recover depends on her experience during childbirth and how quickly her body heals. Some women feel well within a week or two after delivery, while others take months to feel fully recovered. If the mother had an episiotomy, it will take a few weeks or even months to heal completely. If she had a cesarean section, her abdominal incision will take quite some time to heal completely. After six weeks, the mother will return to her health care provider for a checkup to make sure her body has completely recovered from childbirth.

PARENTHOOD

For teens, parenthood is especially difficult. They must give up their own childhood in order to put the baby first. Many teens are raising children with the help of family, friends, boyfriends, community programs, or alone. Many teen moms drop out of high school. They and their

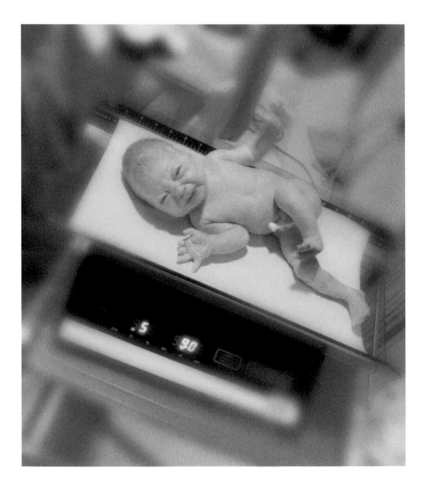

> Do not use breast-feeding as birth control.
> Ovulation and pregnancy can happen when a
> woman breast-feeds, even if she does not get her
> period. If a woman doesn't want to get pregnant
> while breast-feeding, she should use a safe con-
> traceptive.

children will not have good prospects for the future. Some will end up on **welfare**. Because they have so little to look forward to in life, some teens choose parenthood even if it is not in their best interest. Parenthood is a life-changing event.

Most of us look forward to finding a life partner, someone with whom we can share the pleasures, responsibilities, and difficulties of family life. If a parent is going to establish a family with her partner, she may want to consider marriage. Marriage is a serious legal contract binding both partners. Each one accepts legal as well as moral and emotional obligations to the other. Every state has laws about marriage. A couple should consider premarital counseling. Having a child can bring joy, stability, and many other rewards to a relationship. A child can also strain the best relationship. If the commitment between partners is not solid, the relationship may fail.

Before someone decides to single parent, she should ask family and friends for their support. Even with support, single parenting is not easy. It is time-consuming and often complicated and frustrating. The parent can take great pleasure helping the child grow, but there will be no breaks. The child will constantly look to the parent for love and care. As the child's needs change, so will the parent's ability to meet those needs. If the child is ill or

Taking Responsibility

Pregnant and new mothers need to consume plenty of calcium. Milk is one good source.

 114

disabled, even greater effort will be required. It takes years for children to become responsible for themselves.

The parent may become more dependent on her family and friends for help with the child, money, and emotional support. The parent may have to give up a lot of freedom to be a good single parent. On the other hand, she will not have to make compromises with a partner and can raise the child with her values, principles, and beliefs. Parenting requires love, energy, and patience. A person must want to do this for a long time.

Babies are special and most mothers and fathers love their babies. But it is usually easier and healthier for teenagers to wait until they are older to have a baby. It gives the baby and the parents a better chance to have a healthy start together. Teen fathers often share these difficulties. Not all teen fathers accept their responsibility and stay with their partners. Some men deny they are fathers. For a variety of reasons, sometimes the young women or their families reject the fathers' help or involvement. However, many young men do marry or live with their partners and babies and face these difficulties.

Q: When will I be able to fit in my old clothes?

A: Some women can fit in their jeans in a few weeks, but most women take several months. The more extra weight a woman gained during pregnancy, the longer it will take to fit into her regular clothes. This is not the time to diet. To help lose the weight, she should exercise. Taking the baby for a brisk stroll every day is great exercise.

Taking Responsibility

> Mom's House offers free day care as a solution of hope to those faced with difficult choices. This nonprofit licensed day care center serves single parents enrolled in an educational program. As of June 2003, 141 parents have graduated from their respective educational programs. There are thirteen Mom's Houses in the United States.

While the new mother is going through emotional and physical changes, the father will have his own problems. He may feel anxious. Some fathers feel hurt and left out. When those hurt feelings build up, the relationship can end up in trouble. Sometimes a father feels overwhelmed by the responsibilities of the new baby and will tune out and leave everything to the mother. The mother may soon feel abandoned if she has to care for the infant full time. The mother and father need to communicate.

Adoption

Adoption usually occurs when a parent or parents are unable to take care of their newborn baby. The parent decides to have someone else care for, bring up, and love the baby. Pregnant teens who are not ready to be parents have the option to let someone else raise the child. Many women who choose adoption are happy knowing that their children are loved and living in good homes with adults who are eager to be parents.

Fathers also have serious decisions to make about their responsibilities.

Thousands of women and men are waiting to adopt babies.

Adoption is a legal act. The birth parent or parents sign a paper saying they are giving their child to parents who want to and are able to take care of the child. The new adoptive parents agree to raise the child as their own. They also sign the adoption paper in front of a lawyer or a judge. Laws require adoptive parents to pass a home study by a licensed agency or professional. Adoption laws are different in every state, and all adoptions must be approved by a judge.

In an *open adoption*, the names of the birth mother and the adoptive parents are known to one another. The birth mother may select the adoptive parents. She and the adoptive parents may exchange letters and photographs. They may also choose to meet, and also choose to have an ongoing relationship. A *closed adoption* keeps the names of the birth mother and the adoptive parents secret from one another.

Thousands of women and men are waiting to adopt newborn children. Many people choose to adopt children because they are not able to conceive a baby. Some people who can conceive a baby also choose to adopt children. If a person is considering adoption, information and confidential advice are available from adoption agencies or social service departments.

Having a baby when a person is too young can be difficult. Some babies have health problems at birth and as they grow up. Parents often find it hard to care for a baby, especially if they are young teenagers themselves. The teen parents often lose the freedom to do what they want. They find it hard to go out with friends or to get schoolwork done when a baby is around. Teenagers who have babies often drop out of school because they need to work. It may be difficult for teenagers to get a job to pay for food, clothes, toys, and medicine for the baby. The cost of paying someone else to take care of a baby while the parents go to school or work is an additional stress.

Bringing a baby into this world is an important and exciting event. Becoming a parent is one of the biggest changes that can happen to a person. Caring for and loving a child can be a wonderful and amazing experience. It brings with it all sorts of new and different responsibilities. That is why the decision when to start a family is so important.

Boston Children's Hospital, Robert P. Masland, Jr., M.D. and David Estridge (Eds.) *What Teenagers Want to Know About Sex: Questions and Answers.* Boston: Little, Brown and Company, 1988.

Curtis, Glade E., M.D., OB/GYN and Judith Schuler, M.S. *Your Pregnancy Week by Week* (Fourth Edition). Cambridge, Mass.: Perseus Publishing, 2000.

Douglas, Ann. *The Mother of all Pregnancy Books.* Hoboken, N.J.: John Wiley & Sons, 2002.

Eisenberg, Arlene, Heidi E. Murkoff, and Sandee E. Hathaway, B.S.N. *What to Expect the First Year* (Revised). New York: Workman Publishing, 2003.

Eisenberg, Arlene, Heidi E. Murkoff, and Sandee E. Hathaway, B.S.N. *What to Expect When You're Expecting.* New York: Workman Publishing Company, 2002.

Ford-Martin, Paula, with Elisabeth A. Aron, M.D., F.A.C.O.G. *The Everything Pregnancy Book* (Second Edition). Avon, Mass.: Adams Media Corporation, 2003.

Harris, A. Christine Ph.D. *The Pregnancy Journal: A Day-to-Day Guide to a Healthy and Happy Pregnancy.* San Francisco: Chronicle Books, 1996.

Harris, Robie H. *It's Perfectly Normal: Changing Bodies, Growing Up, Sex, and Sexual Health.* Cambridge, Mass.: Candlewick Press, 1994.

Johnson, Eric W. *Love and Sex in Plain Language* (Fourth Revised Edition). New York: Harper & Row Publishers, 1985.

Lees, Christoph, M.D., Karina Reynolds, M.D., and Grainne McCartan. *Pregnancy and Birth: Your Questions Answered.* New York: DK Publishing, 2002.

Lieberman, E. James, M.D., and Karen Lieberman, M.P.H. *Like It Is: A Teen Sex Guide.* Jefferson, N.C.: McFarland & Company Publishers, 1998.

Mucciolo, Gary, M.D. *Everything You Need to Know About Birth Control (The Need to Know Library).* New York: The Rosen Publishing Group, 1996.

Pasquale, Samuel A., M.D., and Jennifer Cadoff. *The Birth Control Book: A Complete Guide to Your Contraceptive Options.* New York: Ballantine Books, 1996.

Stoppard, Miriam, M.D. *Sex Ed: Growing Up, Relationships, and Sex.* New York: DK Publishing, 1997.

Adoption.com
www.adoption.com

Advocates for Youth
www.advocatesforyouth.org/

All About Moms
www.allaboutmoms.com/

Carolinas HealthCare System
healthinfo.carolinas.org/healthtopics/pregnancy.htm

Childbirth.org
www.childbirth.org

National Family Planning and Reproductive Health Association
www.nfprha.org/facts/contraception/

Obstetric Ultrasound
www.ob-ultrasound.net/

Planned Parenthood Federation of America, Inc.
www.ppfa.org/health/

Project Reality
www.projectreality.org/

Safe Place
www.safeplaceservices.org/teentopics/sex.shtml

SHARE (Sexuality, Health, And Relationship Education)
www.share-program.com/teen.htm

Teen Health
www.medill.northwestern.edu/journalism/newme-
dia/Capstone/Group3/index.htm

TeensHealth
kidshealth.org/teen/

anesthesiologist (an-es-THEES-ee-ol-oh-jist) A physician specializing in anesthesia, which are drugs that produce the loss of feeling, especially pain.

cesarean section (suh-SARE-ee-un) The delivery of a baby surgically through the mother's abdomen. Also called C-section.

epidural (ep-i-DER-ul) Injection of a local anesthetic into the epidural space located within the vertebral canal outside the membrane that covers the spinal cord.

episiotomy A straight-cut incision of the mother's perineum (area between vagina and anus) to make the delivery easier.

forceps Metal instruments that fit on either side of the baby's head and are used to help deliver the baby.

genitals The external sex organs.

incontinence Inability to control urination.

induced To have labor started artificially.

lactation The release of milk.

obstetrician A physician specializing in the care of pregnant women.

pediatrician A physician specializing in the care of children.

placenta (pluh-SENT-uh) An organ developing inside the uterus of a pregnant female that is connected to the fetus by the umbilical cord. Made up of tissues from both the fetus and the mother, it allows both of their blood to come into close association for the exchange of respiratory gases, nutrition, and waste products, and it secretes a number of hormones essential for pregnancy.

premature A term that describes an infant that is

born before the normal nine-month term of pregnancy has elapsed.

prenatal Before birth.

puberty The body's transition from childhood to adulthood during which time males and females become capable of reproduction.

quickening The first faint sign of activity of the baby in its mother's womb; usually at about four months.

secondary virginity The decision to abstain from further sexual involvement until marriage. Also called "renewed virginity."

speculum An instrument made of plastic or metal that separates the walls of the vagina so the internal reproductive organs are easy to see.

stillbirths Births of babies after twenty-four weeks of pregnancy, who show no signs of life.

vacuum A hollow tube attached to a plastic or metal cup used to help deliver a baby.

welfare A public agency or program that distributes aid to qualifying disadvantaged social groups.

zygote A single-cell organism.

INDEX

abortion 56
abstinence 24
adoption 13, 51, 60, 67, 116,
    118–119
Apgar score 94

birth control pill 39, 40
breast-feeding 110–111, 113

cesarean section 92, 111
condoms 41–43, 45
contraception, 13, 59
contraception, barrier methods,
    41–45
contraception, behavioral 38–39
contraception, choosing a
    method 47
contraception, emergency 45,
    46–47
contraception, permanent 46
contraceptives, hormonal 39–41
contraceptives, over-the-counter
    37–38
contractions 87, 95

delivery 99–103

fetal alcohol syndrome 83
fetus, development of 68, 73, 78,
    81, 89
first trimester 72–73

herpes 25

labor 95, 97–99
labor, pain of 98

mifepristone (RU-486) 45, 55, 56

natural family planning 38, 47

ovulation 20–21

pregnancy, definition of 53, 67
pregnancy, drugs and 85, 86
pregnancy, healthy diet and
    68–69
pregnancy, physical signs of 54
premature births 88, 92
prenatal care, 56, 59, 64–65,
    69–72, 87
puberty 15, 18, 20

recovery, mother's physical 111
reproductive system 13, 14
reproductive system, female 17,
    18, 20, 21
reproductive system, male 14–16

second trimester 78–81, 83
secondary virginity 29, 105
single parenting 112–113,
    115–116

third trimester 84–89

Artville pp. 10, 32, 54, 65, 71, 74, 90, 107
Brand X pp. 16, 82, 84
Corbis pp. 36, 57
EyeWire pp. 48, 62, 104
iDream pp. 11, 22, 76
Image Source pp. 24, 27, 34, 109
LifeArt pp.14, 51, 52, 66, 79, 86, 89, 99, 101, 101
Masterseries pp. 28, 102
Photodisc pp. 19, 40, 43, 44, 58, 93, 96, 112, 114, 117, 118

The individuals in these images are models, and the images are for illustrative purposes only.

(The author would like to thank the following people for their contributions: Drue Brenner, Director of Education, Planned Parenthood Health Center, Binghamton, New York; Elizabeth Bronson; James Crosby, MD; Kristine P. Cunningham, Executive Administrator, Mom's House, Endicott, New York; Kaley Ehret, Abstinence Program Director, All Women's Help Center, Binghamton, New York; Pat McCoy, Director, Birthright of Binghamton, Johnson City, NY; Karen McMichael, FNP; and Mike Scarinzi, Health Teacher, Vestal Senior High School, Vestal, New York. Special thanks to Project Editor Ellyn Sanna; the author's husband Gary and children: Jonathan, Stephanie, and Christine.)

Donna Lange is a freelance author and editor. In addition to her book *On the Edge of Disaster: Youth in the Juvenile Court System*, her writing appears in magazines and several gift books. She resides in upstate New York with her husband and three teenage children.

Mary Ann McDonnell, APRN, BC, is an advanced practice nurse, the director of the clinical trials program in pediatric psychopharmacology research at Massachusetts General Hospital, has a private practice in pediatric psychopharmacology, and is a clinical instructor for Northeastern University and Boston College advanced practice nursing students. Her areas of expertise are bipolar disorder in children and adolescents, ADHD, and depression. Mary Ann is one of a small group of advanced practice nurses working in pediatric psychopharmacology research and practice, who has a national reputation as an expert advanced practice nurse in the field of pediatric bipolar disorder, ADHD, and depression. She sits on the institutional review board and the research education committee at Massachusetts General Hospital and is a lecturer for local and national educational conferences on bipolar disorder, depression, and ADHD.

Dr. Sara Forman graduated from Barnard College and Harvard Medical School. She completed her residency in Pediatrics at Children's Hospital of Philadelphia and a fellowship in Adolescent Medicine at Children's Hospital Boston (CHB). She currently is an attending in Adolescent Medicine at CHB, where she has served as Director of the Adolescent Outpatient Eating Disorders Program for the past nine years. She has also consulted for the National Eating Disorder Screening Project on its high school initiative and has presented at many conferences about teens and eating disorders. In addition to her clinical and administrative roles in the Eating Disorders Program, Dr. Forman teaches medical students and residents and coordinates the Adolescent Medicine rotation at CHB. Dr. Forman sees primary care adolescent patients in the Adolescent Clinic at CHB, at Bentley College, and at the Germaine Lawrence School, a residential school for emotionally disturbed teenage girls.